PAUL HANCOCK

IS THAT WHAT
YOU MEAN, TOO?
2

50 EVERYDAY IDIOMS AND HOW TO USE THEM

PENGUIN ENGLISH

PENGUIN ENGLISH

Published by the Penguin Group
Penguin Books Ltd, 27 Wrights Lane, London W8 5TZ, England
Penguin Books USA Inc., 375 Hudson Street, New York, New York 10014, USA
Penguin Books Australia Ltd, Ringwood, Victoria, Australia
Penguin Books Canada Ltd, 10 Alcorn Avenue, Toronto, Ontario, Canada M4V 3B2
Penguin Books (NZ) Ltd, 182–190 Wairau Road, Auckland 10, New Zealand

Penguin Books Ltd, Registered Offices: Harmondsworth, Middlesex, England

First published 1992
10 9 8 7 6 5 4 3 2 1

Text copyright © Paul Hancock, 1992
Illustrations copyright © Clive Collins, 1992
All rights reserved
The moral right of the author and illustrator has been asserted
Designed by DW Design Partnership Ltd
Illustrations by Clive Collins

Printed and bound in Great Britain by
BPCC Hazells Ltd

ACKNOWLEDGEMENTS

With particular acknowledgement to Paul Dummet for providing material and helping to get the book finished. Thanks also to Chris Snowdon and Michael Nation for their patience; Kath, Philippa and Sarah for their kindness; John for his perseverance; and the staff and principal of Godmer House School of English for their continuing support.

CONTENTS

INTRODUCTION

To the Student

An idiomatic expression is a group of two or more words which
cannot be understood simply by knowing the meaning of each
separate word – it has a special meaning which speakers of the
language understand. Most learners of English want to and need
to learn some idiomatic expressions because they are such an
important part of the real language we speak.

There are a great many idioms in the English language, and it
is difficult for non-native speakers to know which expressions are
really useful. Many idioms sound quite old-fashioned as they are
not really used very much by English speakers. Some expressions
are so informal or colloquial that it would sound strange if a
foreign speaker used them. The expressions used in this book have,
therefore, been chosen because they are often used by English
speakers, and can also be used quite naturally by foreign learners.

However, learning and using idioms correctly is not easy.
There is the problem of getting them right. An idiomatic
expression must be used absolutely correctly. If you make even
the smallest mistake, the idiomatic expression no longer has its
special meaning. It will actually mean just what the words say,
which is sometimes very strange! The first picture of each
example in this book will show you this and will help to stop you
from making mistakes. Making you aware of these mistakes and
correcting them will make sure that you learn the idiom in its
correct form.

It's often not easy to understand exactly what an idiom
means. The second picture of each example in this book will
help to make the meaning clear. Some more explanation of the
idiom is given under each of these pictures. When you check the
correct answer, notice which word(s) is stressed when the idiom
is spoken. Exercise A in each unit gives further practice in
learning the idioms in their correct form. Exercise B in each unit
will check that you understand which idiom is correct for each
context.

Be sure to remember that very many idioms are informal and that you shouldn't try to use them in a formal context, e.g. writing a letter to a bank manager or the principal of a school. You might think that it would show that your English is very good if you used an idiom in a situation like this, but it can often sound wrong. In this book, therefore, you will be given a way of expressing these ideas in a more formal way. Exercise C in each unit gives you practice in deciding whether idioms sound correct in different contexts. Exercise D is for students who are working in a class. It gives you the opportunity to use the idioms that you have learnt by talking about your personal experiences with someone.

If you are using the book for self-study, the answers to all the exercises can be checked by using the Answers section at the back of the book. This is the best way to use each unit of the book:
1. Look at the pictures and explanations and correct the mistakes.
2. Look at the answers in the back of the book to check that your answers are correct.
3. Do the first practice exercise A. Look again at the pictures and explanations if you are not sure if the practice sentences are right or wrong. Correct the sentences which are wrong.
4. Check your answers to exercise A in the back of the book.
5. Do the practice exercise B. Look at the pictures and explanations again if you are not sure what to write.
6. Check your answers in the back of the book.
7. Do the practice exercise C. Again, look at the explanations if you are not sure which answer to choose.
8. Check your answers in the back of the book.

Exercise D is for classroom use only.

To the Teacher

The introduction to the student explains the value of *Is That What You Mean, Too?* to learners of English who would like to get a good understanding of some widely used idiomatic expressions (including some phrasal verbs). The book is for students at intermediate and advanced level. As well as focusing on the correct form and meaning of a selection of idioms, each unit helps students to see whether they can use the idioms in different registers. There is also a free production exercise at the end of each unit in which students can use the expressions in a personal context. Those teachers who have used *Is That What You Mean?* will see that this book can be used in class in a similar way.

A suggested method of using each unit of the book in class:

1. Put the students in pairs or groups. Ask them to look through the pictures and explanations and to correct the mistakes.
2. When they have finished, check the correct form of the idiom as a class, and practise speaking the sentence with the correct stress pattern (as shown in the Index of Idioms – page 132). The illustration of the incorrect idiom often shows the literal meaning. The illustration of the correct idiom should be used to check that students have got its meaning correct. You can do this by asking questions about what the people in the illustrations are doing and why, e.g. page 80 'How does the teacher look? Why? Why do you think the hotel manager doesn't understand his French? Do the children feel sorry for the teacher? What will happen when the teacher next tries to correct his students' French?' The illustration can also be used to introduce extra vocabulary if you wish (e.g. page 80, *to frown, to shrug your shoulders, to check in, hotel lobby,* etc). You could ask the students now to provide a clear definition of the idiom in simple language (a list is provided on page 132). Check that students have an idea of how formal the expression is and ask a student to give the more formal alternative.
3. Ask the students to do exercise A in pairs or groups. You could teach or check any vocabulary which your class might not know. When they have finished, check the answers as a class.

4. Repeat the same procedure with exercise B. Encourage the students first to try and remember the idiom without looking back at the presentation pages. You can go round while they are doing the exercise and make sure that all students have written the idiom in its correct form.

5. Go through the introduction to exercise C with all the students. Then ask them to do the exercise in pairs or groups. There may be a lot of quite difficult vocabulary for lower level students in the formal sentences. This can be taught or checked, but it isn't actually necessary that they understand everything in these sentences. What is more important is that they get the basic meaning of them and recognize them as formal in context and language. Check the answers as a class again, dealing with difficult vocabulary if you wish.

6. Exercise D is free production practice. This exercise could be done after the others or at a later time for revision.

    Write out the idioms practised in each unit (see Index of Idioms, page 132) on pieces of paper and give them to the students. Students could work in pairs and prepare five or six idioms each. Alternatively, in a larger group each student could prepare fewer idioms, or in a group of 10 or 12 people, each student could prepare one idiom each. Each student has to prepare to talk about a personal experience, which would get a partner or another member of the group to produce the idiom on their piece of paper. The other student(s) can then ask more questions about the personal experience. An example is given in each unit. Students will need some time to prepare their answers and you can help with any difficulties, such as vocabulary. Monitor the students if they are working in pairs or groups, and make sure that they use the idiom with correct stress and intonation. If students work in pairs or groups, you could ask each student afterwards quickly to tell the class the most interesting story they heard from their partner or the person next to them in their group, using the idiom of course.

1

**'Mr and Mrs Doubleday are not very good parents
– they never put their feet down.'**

Even though you are talking about two people here (and four
feet!), you must always use the singular when you use this
expression.

**'Mr and Mrs Doubleday are not very good parents
– they never ....'**

If you do what this expression suggests, it means that
someone has been behaving badly towards you and that you
have accepted it, but that now you've had enough. You do or
say something to show that you are definitely not going to
accept this behaviour any more.

This is quite an informal expression. A more formal way of
expressing the same idea is *to assert one's authority*,
e.g. 'Teachers who do not assert their authority over a class of
difficult students at the beginning will find it impossible to
regain control later.'

**'Valerie's new boyfriend is definitely in love with
her – he gives a ring to her every evening.'**

The expression you need here means the same as *to telephone/to
phone/to call*. With these verbs, and with this expression, you
have to say who you are telephoning immediately after the
verb, but without *to*.

'Valerie's new boyfriend is definitely in love with her – he .... every evening.'

This is one of the most popular ways of saying *to telephone* when you are speaking or writing informally. It is used especially when you are asking someone to phone you in the future, or offering to phone them. You can also use *a call* instead of *a ring*.

This is a fairly informal expression. A more formal way of saying the same thing is *to telephone (someone)*, e.g. 'Yes. Mr Chadwick. I will give Mr Allan your message as soon as he returns and ask him to telephone you.'

3

**'Clare can't put up Ashley's motorbike any longer
– it's too noisy.'**

To put up means *to provide accommodation for someone.* E.g. 'If you
can't find a cheap hotel, we can put you up for a few days.'
Here you need to use another preposition after *up* to get the
phrasal verb with the right meaning.

'Clare can't .... Ashley's motorbike any longer – it's too noisy.'

This phrasal verb means *to tolerate* or *to stand*. You might tolerate something which annoys you for as long as you can, even though you don't like it. When you can't stand it any longer, you decide to put a stop to it.

This is an informal, but commonly used expression. A formal expression for the same idea is *to tolerate*,
e.g. Dear Mr Larkins,
The reason that you have been dismissed from your job is that the company does not tolerate lateness.

4

'Dave and Helen managed to reach the theatre before the opera started, but it was a race against the time.'

You use the definite article with *time* when you are asking about the information you get from a clock or watch, e.g. 'What's the time? / Have you got the right time, please?' Here you don't need to use the article because you are talking about time in a general sense, as something which always exists.

'Dave and Helen managed to reach the theatre before the opera started, but it was ....'

This can be used in any situation where you have to do something which is important, and which must be done by a definite time (a deadline). It's often used about work, when you must complete something before a deadline. You can't use it as a verb (i.e. *to race*), only as a noun – you always say 'it was/is/will be *a race* against . . .'

This expression is used formally as well as informally.

5

**'I couldn't remember his name when he arrived,
but it was on the end of my tongue.'**

You have to use another word for *end* here – the word which is
usually used to describe the very end of something, e.g. your
finger, toe, nose or tongue.

**'I couldn't remember his name when he arrived,
but it was on the ....'**

You use this expression when you know something, usually a
name, word or number, and you feel as if you are going to be
able to say it any moment. However, you can't quite
remember it.

This expression is usually used informally. You can give a
similar meaning in a more formal way with *not quite be able to
remember*,

e.g. 'Mr Siddle, who is accused of receiving stolen goods, told
the police that he knew the name of the man who sold him
the videos but that he wasn't quite able to remember it.'

6

'We keep trying to find time to visit you, but the dogs tie us up most evenings.'

This is the right expression but you can only use it in the *passive form.* Otherwise it means *to put rope or string around (someone/something).* You also have to make sure you use the right preposition after the passive – if you use *by*, this picture would still be true!

'We keep trying to find time to visit you, but we .... most evenings.'

This can be used to talk about any activity, hobby or work which occupies a lot of your time, so that you are not free to do other things. If you use it without saying what the activity is, it's an informal way of saying that you are not free at the moment.

This is only used as an informal expression. A more formal expression for the same idea is *to be occupied (with)*, e.g. 'The Queen thanks you for your kind invitation but regrets that she will be occupied with another engagement that day.'

**'When the new cook started work, Maurizio was
always pulling his legs.'**

You need the singular form in this expression.

'When the new cook started work, Maurizio was always ....'

This expression means *to play a joke* on someone, *to tease* them. You tell them something unpleasant or worrying which isn't in fact true. If they believe it and get worried, then you show that it is a joke and everyone has a laugh about it. It's a friendly joke, and not one you can make about very serious things that could upset people.

(If you think someone is doing this to you, and you want to show that you don't believe what they are saying, you can say, 'Pull the other one!')

This is an informal expression. There is no real formal way of saying the same thing, because it is not something which is done in a formal context.

**'I arrived twenty minutes after the film had
started, but Richard soon put me into the picture.'**

You normally use *into* with verbs of movement, e.g. 'go into',
'come into'. The preposition you need here is similar,
but shorter.

'I arrived twenty minutes after the film had started, but Richard soon ....'

We use this expression when someone has missed the beginning of something, e.g. an event or film, and needs to have an explanation of what has happened so far. We do this so that the person can understand what is happening and follow what is going to happen next.

This is a fairly informal expression. A more formal way of expressing the same idea is *to explain the background (to someone)*, e.g. 'Before I go any further I think I should explain to the court the background to the events of the night of 25 June.'

9

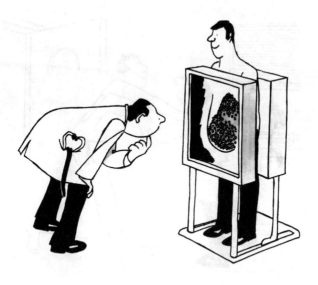

**'The doctor could see that James was filled with
beans when he came for the medical examination.'**

To be filled with is the passive form of *to fill*. It is often used to
describe how something is made, e.g. 'The cakes are left for 30
minutes to cool and then filled with cream.' Here you need
the adjective which is the opposite of *empty*, with its usual
preposition.

**'The doctor could see that James was ....
when he came for the medical examination.'**

You use this expression to describe someone who is very lively
and full of energy. (They may not always be like this.) Often
you use it to ask someone what has happened to make them
so full of life.

This is an informal expression. A more formal way of saying
the same thing is *to be in high spirits*,
e.g. 'Although Mr Ogansoy may have to pay over £1 million if
he is found guilty of tax fraud, he was in high spirits when he
spoke to journalists at today's press conference.'

**'It's sad that so many wild animals are overrun by
cars these days.'**

When animals or plants *overrun* a place, they fill it completely
with their great numbers, e.g. 'The city of Hamelin was
overrun by rats.' You can also say that a place is 'overrun by
tourists'. It can be used formally or informally. The phrasal
verb you need here is two separate words, with the
preposition second.

**'It's sad that so many wild animals are ....
by cars these days.'**

This means that you hit something or knock it down, while
you are driving a motor vehicle or riding a motorbike. Your
wheels then go over it. The thing that you hit can come before
or after the preposition.

This expression can be used in both a formal and an informal
context, but when used about people it can sound too direct.
So there is another more formal way of saying the same thing,
which is *to be hit (by a car, lorry, etc.)*,
e.g. 'A man and his wife died tragically when they were hit by
a lorry while walking their dog to the park yesterday
afternoon.'

UNIT ONE

Decide whether the following sentences are right or wrong. If a sentence is wrong, correct it.

1. Your boss will keep giving you more and more extra work, unless you put your foot down now.
2. If I manage to get tickets for the concert tonight, I'll give a ring to you and let you know.
3. I don't know how Astrid can put up the noise of traffic all day.
4. We have to start work on another house next Tuesday, so finishing this one is going to be a race against time.
5. Oh, I wish I could remember the name of that village we stayed in. It's on the top of my tongue.
6. I'm afraid I won't be able to come to basketball practice this week – I'm tied up with exam marking.
7. Pam, don't look so worried. Roger's only pulling your legs.
8. Well, I hope you had a good holiday. We've been having problems with our agent in Paris while you've been away, but Colin will put you into the picture about it all.
9. Kate is filled with beans today. Is her boyfriend back from abroad?
10. Mrs Jones is very worried about her son walking to school because three children have already been run over this year.
11. If some of you don't mind sleeping on the floor, we can put you all up.
12. The Acropolis in Athens is overrun by tourists in the summer months.

Complete the following sentences, using one of the idiomatic expressions from this unit.

1. I never know whether to believe anything Stan tells me because he is always ....

2. When is your brother leaving? I don't think I can .... his terrible jokes any longer.

3. Imogen left a message on the answerphone. She asked if you could .... later to tell her what time Patrick is arriving.

4. I asked Christine if she was free any weekend in September, but she is very .... with work when the new school term starts.

5. I don't understand. We were both at the party until 2 o'clock this morning and we both had three hours' sleep. How is it that I'm half dead and you're so .... ?

6. One of our cats was .... by a car, but we still have the other one.

7. That company sent taxis late three times in one week, so we .... and said we would use another taxi company if in future they didn't come on time.

8. I couldn't give the answer to the last question on the TV quiz show, even though it was on the ....

9. We must make sure we set off early for the airport. I don't want it to be a ....

10. You're late again, Ali! The class are in the middle of an activity, but if you work with Sylvia's group she'll ....

11. If you don't mind sleeping on the sofa, I can .... at my house.

12. The house was a complete mess when we moved in and the basement was .... by mice.

 In this unit, as you have seen, some of the idiomatic expressions are informal or even very informal, but others can be used in both a formal and an informal context. This exercise gives you practice in choosing the right expression for different contexts.

In each question below, first decide who you think is speaking or where you would read the item. Then choose from the possibilities in the brackets either the idiomatic expression or the more formal way of saying the same thing. N.B. Although

it is often true that formal English is written and informal English spoken, this is not always necessarily true.

1. Mr Greene, who is eighty-seven and has just published his fifty-second novel, was (full of beans/in high spirits) yesterday when he gave an interview to waiting journalists.

2. 'This is the Central Electricity Board. Unfortunately the office is closed until Monday. If you would like to leave your name and telephone number, one of our service personnel will (give you a ring/telephone you) as soon as possible.'

3. INFORMATION FOR CONFERENCE PARTICIPANTS
Several local organizers may be able to (put participants up/provide accommodation for participants) in their homes, but this will be on a limited basis only. Participants are advised to seek alternative accommodation in local hotels, a list of which is available on request.

4. 'Alan, I want to have a word with you about Yvonne. I know she is a good friend of yours, but I'm really fed up with her using the phone all the time to make long-distance calls. I'm going to have to (put my foot down/assert my authority) and tell her she has to pay in future.'

5. 'And now the local news. An elderly woman was (run over/hit) by a car outside Hornsea town hall this morning. Her condition is described as critical.'

6. Before continuing with this book's analysis of the October revolution, and the events which followed it, it will be necessary to (put the reader in the picture about/explain to the reader the background to) the social and political mood of the time.

7. 'Mrs Sweeney for Dr Otterburn? I'm afraid Dr Otterburn is still (tied up with/occupied with) another patient and I wouldn't like to disturb him. Would you mind telephoning again in about half an hour?'

8. 'To be honest, I don't really like the radio on while I'm working. But I suppose I could (put up with/tolerate) it for half an hour, as it's your favourite programme.'

9. 'I wish you'd never asked me the name of that actor. (His name has been on the tip of my tongue/I haven't been able to remember his name) all day, and it's driving me mad.'

10. 'Hello Diane, this is Simon. I'm coming down to Exeter for a job interview next week and wondered if you could (put me up/provide accommodation for me) for a couple of days.'

Your teacher will give you one or more idioms from this unit to work with. For each idiom, think about a time when you (or someone you know or have heard about) had the experience which this idiom describes.

Prepare some notes so that you can tell another student about this experience. (Ask your teacher for help with any vocabulary you need.) The important thing is that you **mustn't use the idiom** *when you are talking.*

When you have talked about the experience, the other student(s) should be able to produce the idiom, and they can then ask you some questions about what happened.

Look at this example for the idiom **to put up with**.

Student A: My younger sister started playing the violin when she was eight – that was four years ago. She wasn't very good and she used to practise at home a lot. She made an awful noise sometimes. After a few months my mother told her that she would have to go into the garage if she wanted to practise.

Student B: So, your mother couldn't put up with it any more?

Student A: That's right.

Student B: And did your sister practise in the garage?

Student A: Yes, she . . .

Student B: Does she play the violin now?

Student A: Yes, she still . . .

etc.

1

**'He was worried before the exam, but for him it
was a piece of a cake.'**

When we talk about a portion of food we generally don't use
an article before the name of the food, e.g. 'a slice of bread, a
leg of chicken', etc.

**'He was worried before the exam, but for him it
was a ....'**

This expression means that you find something very easy. We
often use it to make someone feel better when they are worried
that a thing will be difficult for them.

This is only used informally. A formal way of expressing this
idea is *(to be) very easy,*
e.g. 'It was very easy to find people who agreed with the idea
of this project, but more difficult to get financial support.'

2

'It takes Bill a long time to show his holiday
slides – he keeps being carried away.'

If you use the verb *to be* here, you are using the passive. For
this expression, you don't need the passive, but the verb
which is used informally to mean *become*. (It can *sometimes* be
used informally to make a passive, but not here.)

**'It takes Bill a long time to show his holiday
slides – he keeps ....'**

This is what can happen when you have very strong feelings
about what you are saying or doing. You can lose your self-
control and behave in a way that is not correct for
the situation.

This is a fairly informal expression. A more formal way of
saying the same thing is *to become overenthusiastic*,
e.g. 'The tendency among players to become overenthusiastic
and use abusive language on the football field is one of the
causes of bad behaviour among football supporters.'

3

**'When Philippa was decorating her house she
broke her arm, but she was lucky to have friends
she could fall back onto.'**

You often use *to fall* with *onto* because it is a verb of
movement. You could say 'she fell back onto the bed'. But in
this expression you are not really talking about someone
falling and after *back* you need a similar, but shorter
preposition.

'When Philippa was decorating her house she broke her arm, but she was lucky to have friends she could ....'

This means that you can rely on someone to help you when you are in a difficult situation. Perhaps you have tried to manage on your own, but now you need help. (You can imagine that someone would be behind you and catch you if you did fall!) You can also use this for things, e.g. an old car which you could use if your new car didn't start.

This expression is used informally. A formal expression which gives the same idea is *to rely on in case of need*, e.g. 'The second parachute is there to rely on in case of need. If the main parachute should fail to open, you will find that this second one opens automatically.'

4

**'I see that Mr and Mrs Davis have finally met their
matches on the tennis court.'**

Although you are talking about two people here, you always
use the singular with this expression.

'I see that Mr and Mrs Davis have finally ....
on the tennis court.'

You use this expression when someone who does something
well meets someone who is as good as, or better than, they
are. It is usually a bit of a shock to them to finally meet some
serious competition.

This is a fairly informal expression. A more formal expression
with a similar meaning is *to find an equal*,
e.g. 'At the small village school where Sir John was educated,
he was used to being top of his class. It was therefore a
surprise to him to find an equal so soon after arriving at
university.'

5

**'Mrs Johnson said she was glad to see Karl's
back.'**

You can't use the usual *'s* form of the possessive when you use
this expression. You have to use the possessive form with *of*,
and you will also need to put the definite article before *back*.

'Mrs Johnson said she was glad to see ....'

The word *back* is used in this expression because that is the part of someone (or something) that you see when they leave you. If you are glad to see this, it means that you have had enough of them. It is also possible to use other words, which mean *glad*, e.g. *happy*, *pleased*, etc.

This is an informal expression. A formal way of saying the same thing is *to be relieved/glad when someone/something (leaves/is removed, etc.)*,
e.g. 'The population of Moscow were glad when the statue was removed. It had stood for over 40 years as a symbol of a political regime which they disliked and feared.'

6

'Paul will have to come back down to the earth one day.'

You always use the definite article *the* with *earth* when you are talking about the planet as we see it from space. In this expression, however, you don't use any article.

'Paul will have to .... one day.'

This expression is used for people who are dreamers or for people who do not (or do not *want* to) see things as they really are. We often use it to say we want them to stop dreaming. You can use it without the word 'back' if you think that someone has *never* seen things as they really are!

This expression is informal. If you want to say the same thing in a more formal way, use *to accept reality*, e.g. 'As a society we have believed for some time that economic and industrial growth can continue without limits. We have to accept reality now and acknowledge that the environment cannot support such unlimited growth.'

7

'This music brings me back to the time I spent in Greece.'

You can use *bring* with this expression, but only if you leave out the *me* and the *to*, e.g. 'This music brings back the time I spent in Greece'. It is more often used with the verb which is the opposite of *bring*. Then you use *me/him/her* etc, before the word *back*, and *to* after it. Use it like this for the correct picture.

'This music .... the time I spent in Greece.'

Many things can do this to you, e.g. music, smells, food, etc.
They make you remember past experiences, or a particular
period in your life very clearly so that you can almost imagine
being there again. The experience or time you remember is
often in the distant past.

This is a fairly informal expression. A formal expression with
a similar meaning is *to evoke memories of*,
e.g. 'The story is seen through the eyes of a child and the
author describes this child's way of looking at the world so
effectively that it will automatically evoke memories of the
reader's own childhood.'

8

**'Don't worry about Sharon and Wayne arguing –
it's just a storm in a cup of tea.'**

You use only one word here to describe what you drink tea
from. This is because it hasn't really got tea in it in this
expression. In the same way we talk about *a pot of tea*, when it
is full, but when it is empty it is *a teapot*; or we say *a bottle of
milk* but when it is empty we say *milk bottle*.

**'Don't worry about Sharon and Wayne arguing –
it's just a ....'**

If there really was a storm in such a small container, it would be a very small storm. This expression describes an argument or problem between people which seems very big and serious at first. However, it is not about anything very important and will probably be finished quickly.

This is an informal and rather colloquial expression. A formal way of saying the same thing is *unnecessary commotion*, e.g. 'The Prime Minister said yesterday that the rise in unemployment was only a temporary setback for the government, implying that there had been a lot of unnecessary commotion about it.'

9

**'The only trouble with teaching that class is
Marcel – he's always splitting hair.'**

If you use the uncountable form of the noun *hair*, it means the
hair on someone's head. In this expression we are talking
about just a few hairs, so you need the countable plural form.

'The only trouble with teaching that class is Marcel – he's always ....'

This expression means that someone insists that every fact people use is correct. They will argue about very small and unimportant things, when most people would agree that it doesn't really matter.

This is an informal expression, usually only used when speaking. The formal expression is *to be pedantic*, e.g. 'Although the legal language in a contract may appear to be pedantic, it is necesary for it to be written in this way in order to protect both parties involved.'

10

**'I ran over Giles in town yesterday. It was great to
see him again.'**

To *run over* someone means to hit them when you are driving a
car or other motor vehicle (see p. 20). To form the correct
phrasal verb here, you need a different preposition.

'I .... Giles in town yesterday. It was great
to see him again.'

This means that you meet someone you know by chance in a
public place, usually when you are out walking somewhere. If
you use this same phrasal verb for someone driving a car, it
means that the car hits something, but the wheels don't go
over it.

This is an informal expression. A formal way of expressing the
same idea is *to meet by chance*,
e.g. 'When the two ex-lovers, who separated after the making
of the film *Running Scared*, met by chance in the Ritz Hotel
yesterday, they refused to speak to each other.'

PRACTICE

UNIT TWO

 ***Decide whether these sentences are right or wrong. If a
sentence is wrong, correct it.***

1. Don't worry about your driving test – it'll be a piece of cake.

2. Please have some more soup. There was only supposed to be
enough for four people, but I was carried away when I was making
it.

3. Of course I find it hard to manage sometimes, but if I'm in
financial trouble I know I can always fall back on my parents.

4. I didn't think anyone else could eat as much as we do, but we
certainly met our matches in Pat and Jack.

5. Paul has had so many problems with that car – he'll be glad to see
its back.

6. He thinks that everything is going really well in the business, but
he'll soon come down to earth when he sees how much money we've
lost.

7. Mmm! Fresh sunflower-seed bread! This takes me back to when I
lived in Germany.

8. Franco and Audrey are having one of their usual arguments about
who should do the shopping. It's just a storm in a teacup.

9. He's Scottish, not English. I'm not just splitting hairs – it's an
important difference.

10. I hope I don't run over Paul if I go into town. I owe him £10.

11. The escaped gorilla fell asleep after eating the drugged food and
was carried away by two men from the zoo.

12. I'm sorry about your car. I'm afraid I ran over a tree at the end of
the road.

B *Complete the following sentences using the expressions you have practised in this unit.*

1. What does it matter whether the score was 21/17 or 21/18? I won, and .... about the score isn't going to change that.

2. Stan! Just calm down! Whenever you start discussing politics, you always .... and start shouting at people.

3. What? Imogen seriously thinks she's going to make £20,000 a year selling books door-to-door? She'll .... with a bump when she starts the job!

4. Mother, I'm in a very difficult situation. I'm sorry I haven't rung you for a long time, but I know you're someone I can .... at a time like this.

5. Your brother talks a lot! Still, he'll .... when my sister arrives – she never stops talking!

6. It's incredible. We hadn't seen Christoph and Katja for three years, and then we .... them in the middle of London!

7. I always enjoy listening to Beatles' records. It .... when I was a teenager in 1966.

8. I don't think Pam will be angry with you for very long – it's just a ....

9. My students this term have been terrible. I'll certainly be glad to .... them on Friday.

10. Everybody told me that finding a job in Spain would be really difficult, but in fact it was .... !

11. I was standing just on the edge of the road and a cyclist .... my foot.

12. I wasn't driving very fast, but I didn't notice the traffic lights change to red, and I .... the back of a bus.

The idiomatic expressions you have learnt in this unit are all normally used in informal contexts. This exercise gives you practice in choosing the correct expression for different contexts. In each question below, first decide who you think is speaking, or where you would read the item. Then choose from the possibilities in the brackets either the idiomatic expression or the more formal way of saying the same thing. N.B. Although it is often true that formal English is written and informal English spoken, this is not always necessarily true.

1. 'Do sit down, Mr Krypke. Did you have any trouble finding our offices?'
    'No, thank you. It was (a piece of cake/very easy).'

2. Mr Rigsby has been a keen and motivated salesman and would be an asset to any team. However, he can (get carried away/become overenthusiastic) at times and apply his sales techniques a little too forcefully.

3. Two fire extinguishers are located on every floor so that should one fail there is always another (to fall back on/to rely on in case of need).

4. 'Iron' Mike Tyson, who has been at the top of world boxing for so long finally (met his match/found an equal) tonight at the Albert Hall.

5. 'Were you sorry about Mr Johnson's resignation?'
    'One is always sorry when a close friend resigns, but for the sake of the party and the government I am (glad to see the back of him/relieved that he has left).'

6. 'Those employees who have decided to take industrial action will have to (come back down to earth/accept reality) – if they continue to strike, they will forfeit their jobs.'

7. 'That was a lovely wedding, wasn't it?'
    'Yes, it was. Doesn't it (take you back to/evoke memories of) our wedding all those years ago?'

8. The Minister for Health said that all this media attention to one isolated case of food poisoning in a hospital was (a storm in a teacup/an unnecessary commotion).

9. 'I think Finnish is the most difficult European language to learn.'
    'Well actually it isn't European – it's not part of the Indo-European language group.'
    'Oh, for goodness sake! There's no need to (split hairs/be pedantic)! You know what I meant.'

10. The two men who committed the robbery were, in fact, old work colleagues. They (ran into each other/met by chance) again two weeks ago in a pub in south London, from where they planned and executed the crime.

Your teacher will give you one or more idioms from this unit to work with. For each idiom, think about a time when you (or someone you know or have heard about) had the experience which this idiom describes.

Prepare some notes so that you can tell another student about this experience. (Ask your teacher for help with any vocabulary you need.) The important thing is that you **mustn't use the idiom** *when you are talking.*

When you have talked about the experience, the other student(s) should be able to use the idiom, and can then ask you some questions about what happened.

Look at this example for the idiom **to run over**.

Student A: There was a terrible accident last year on the road near where I live. A man and his wife were walking home from the cinema. Suddenly a car came around the corner very fast and hit the man. The driver didn't stop, but drove away fast and the woman had to go to the nearest house to get help.

Student B: You mean, the driver ran over him?

Student A: Yes, that's right.

Student B: And was he badly injured?

Student A: Yes, both his legs . . .

Student B: Did the police ever catch the driver?

etc.

1

**'I haven't seen Jimmy for ages. Next time I'm in
Scotland I must look up him.'**

For the meaning you need here, you need to change the word
order. A name, or the pronoun *me/him/her*, should come *between*
the verb and the preposition.

(You can also use this phrasal verb when you want to find
or check a piece of information. If you use it with this
meaning, there are two possible orders with a noun phrase,
e.g. 'look *the word* up in the dictionary' or 'look up *the word* in
the dictionary', but with a pronoun, it must come *between* the
verb and the preposition, e.g. 'look *it* up.')

**'I haven't seen Jimmy for ages. Next time I'm in
Scotland I must ....'**

This means to visit an old friend you have not seen for a long
time when you go to a place where they live. The visit might
or might not be the reason for your going to this place.

This is an informal expression and can only be used with
someone you know well. You can give a similar meaning with
to visit someone you haven't seen for a long time.

2

**'When we got to the holiday homes, the manager
told us to take our picks.'**

This kind of *pick* (a tool used for breaking stone) is a
countable noun (plural = *picks*). Here you need the
uncountable noun, which has no plural form.

**'When we got to the holiday homes, the manager
told us to ....'**

This expression uses the noun form of the verb *to pick*, which means *to choose*. It's often used when you are buying something and you are invited to choose whichever thing you want.

This is an informal expression. A formal way of saying the same thing is *to select the (thing) of your choice*, e.g. 'We offer a range of bathrooms to suit your particular taste and needs. Customers are invited to select the bathroom of their choice and we will do the rest – planning, delivery and fitting.'

3

**'I'll have to lose some weight because this is
becoming a vicious cycle.'**

We use the word *cycle* in two ways. Firstly as an abbreviation
of *bicycle*, e.g. 'a cycle path', 'a cycle shop', and secondly as a
series of things which happen repeatedly, e.g. 'The cycle of the
seasons' is spring, summer, autumn and winter. Here you
need a similar, but different word. (It's the same word we use
to describe the round shape you might draw on paper.)

'I'll have to lose some weight because this is becoming ....'

This describes the way in which we can get stuck in our problems. We try to solve a problem in a way that actually creates another problem. So our solution leads us back to the original problem and we cannot escape.

This is an expression which we use in both formal and informal situations. Another possibility for formal contexts would be *a self-perpetuating problem*. Generally it sounds better to use the idiomatic expression.

4

**'I'd forgotten that Mrs Matthews' sister died last
month, so when I asked who the photograph was
of, I really put my foot on it.'**

If you stand on something you put your foot (or feet) *on* it. In
this expression you use a different preposition, which suggests
that your foot enters something.

**'I'd forgotten that Mrs Matthews' sister died last
month, so when I asked who the photograph was
of, I really ....'**

You always use *it* after the preposition with this expression.
We use this expression to describe a situation when there is
some difficult or embarrassing subject which it would be
better *not* to talk about, but which someone (or you!) *does* talk
about, or draws attention to. By doing this you can make
someone embarrassed, upset or angry unnecessarily.

This is an informal expression. The formal way to express the
same idea is *to make a tactless remark*,
e.g. 'I was sorry to hear that one of our reporters made a
tactless remark at the local conference for disabled people. As
editor of the 'Eastmoor Express' I can only hope that you will
accept my sincere apologies on behalf of the newspaper.'

5

'Geoff and Jude usually organize a few games to break ice at their parties.'

When we talk about ice for drinks we usually use no article.
In this expression we use the definite article.

'Geoff and Jude usually organize a few games to
.... at their parties.'

If people don't know each other at a party, they often feel
uncomfortable at the beginning, so the atmosphere is 'cold'.
This expression describes the things people do at the
beginning of parties, conferences and courses to help everyone
get to know each other and 'warm up'.

This is a fairly informal expression. A more formal way of
saying the same thing is *to create a more congenial atmosphere*,
e.g. 'The two leaders spent an hour over coffee this morning.
This helped to create a more congenial atmosphere before the
serious talks started in the afternoon'.

6

**'Mr Sturgess is going to overtake Mr Simpson's
position as manager.'**

As well as for driving on the road, *to overtake* is used in
sports, like running, or horseracing. It can also be used in
other situations where you get in front of someone after
being behind,
e.g. 'Britain used to be one of the most successful economies
in Europe, but many European countries have now
overtaken it.'
The phrasal verb you need here is two separate words, with
the preposition second.

'Mr Sturgess is going to .... Mr Simpson's position as manager.'

For a job or activity in a firm, this verb means that a new person is going to do the job. You can use this expression in two ways: 'Mr Smith will . . . Mr Jones' position as headmaster', or 'Mr Smith will . . . *from* Mr Jones as headmaster'.

For other activities it can mean that a new person is going to do the activity because the other person is tired, or would like a change. It is also used when a large company buys another, smaller company.

This expression is used both formally and informally.

7

'I learnt how to make Turkish coffee quite easily, but making an Italian espresso was a completely different kettle of fishes.'

The noun *fish* does have a plural *fishes*, but it is not used often. We normally use the irregular plural which, like *sheep*, doesn't change form when you make it plural.

'I learnt how to make Turkish coffee quite easily, but making an Italian espresso was a completely ....'

We use this expression when someone expects two things to be similar, but in fact they are different. The expression tells them that the second thing may be more difficult for them than they imagine. We often use it to warn people about this.

This is an informal expression. A formal way of saying the same thing is *another matter altogether*, e.g. 'Diving at ten metres presents few problems to the inexperienced diver, but diving at thirty metres is another matter altogether.'

8

'My brother hit the ceiling when I told him that I'd crashed his car.'

The ceiling is the top of the room you are in, but for this expression you use the word that means the very top of the house.

'My brother .... when I told him that I'd crashed his car.'

This means that someone suddenly lets out a lot of anger, like a rocket firing into the air. It happens with some people when you tell them some bad news, or when you do something that upsets them.

This is an informal and colloquial expression. To express the same idea in a formal context, use *to explode with anger*, e.g. 'It is said that when Mr MacGregor heard that a newspaper had got hold of his confidential report, he exploded with anger and immediately telephoned the editor to tell him not to publish the story.'

9

**'It was nearly 9.20 a.m., but only one person in
the office had got down for work.'**

Get down usually means to come down from a high place. You
can say that you are 'ready *for* work' or 'late *for* work', but
with this phrasal verb you need a different preposition
after *down*.

'It was nearly 9.20 a.m., but only one person in the office had .... work.'

This expression means that you really start working in a serious way. This is sometimes not an easy thing to do, and before doing it, people often spend a lot of time doing other unimportant things, or daydreaming. We usually use this expression in connection with work or something that has to be done (e.g. writing a letter).

This is a fairly informal expression. We can express the same idea in a much more formal way by using *to start (work etc.)*, e.g. 'Before starting the repair of the puncture, ensure that you have all the necessary tools ready to hand. You will need a 13mm spanner, . . .'

10

**'Can you keep the eye on the soup? I'm just going
to make a phone call.'**

In English we don't normally use *the* with parts of the body
when we refer to a part of a particular person's body. Instead
we use the possessive pronoun (e.g. 'He broke *his* arm', 'She
has lost *her* voice'). With this expression you could use the
possessive pronoun or the indefinite article. (You must use the
singular form of the noun.)

'Can you .... the soup? I'm just going to make a phone call.'

We use this expression when we want someone to look after something for us because we are not going to be there to look after it for ourselves (e.g. food which is cooking, children playing outside). The person who is asked to do this should check from time to time that everything is OK.

This is an informal expression. A formal way of saying the same thing is *to monitor*,

e.g. 'Now you have planted and watered the tree you should monitor its progress for a few weeks to make sure that it has taken to the soil and that no diseases develop.'

UNIT THREE

 Decide whether these sentences are right or wrong. If a sentence is wrong, correct it.

1. Why don't you look Sarah up in Ipswich if you're going to a meeting there?

2. We prefer to buy vegetables from the supermarket, because then we can take our picks.

3. Heroin users become more and more unhappy, and then need more of the drug to make them feel better, so it becomes a vicious cycle.

4. Do you think I put my foot on it when I asked Rosie if she'd bought the cake from a shop?

5. The first day of a new course is difficult for students and teachers. You really need a few games or activities to break the ice.

6. I'm going to start the presentation by talking about Tibet, and then Rosemary will take over and show you some photographs of her visit.

7. I thought the fact that I used to play the guitar might help, but learning to play the piano is a different kettle of fishes altogether.

8. Don't tell mum I didn't get in till 11.00 last night – she'll hit the roof if she finds out!

9. I've been sitting and reading the newspaper all morning. I just can't seem to get down for work.

10. Harriet asked Peter to keep the eye on Robert and Eli while she went to the shop to get them an ice-cream.

11. Rachel, could you look these words up in the French dictionary for me?

12. '. . . and as they come round the corner into the last 200 metres, Rogers is taking over the Kenyan runner in the outside lane.'

B *Complete the following sentences using the expressions you have practised in this unit.*

1. Hello Kutlu! Listen, I'm coming to Istanbul for a course next week, and I'd like to .... while I'm there.

2. Denise is leaving us next month, so Maggie will be .... as accommodation secretary.

3. I didn't think Simon would be angry when I told him I'd lost his cassette, but he nearly .... !

4. We all arrive at work at about 9.15 on Monday mornings, but it's usually about 10.00 before we finally .... work.

5. I know she doesn't want to go out much in the depressed state she's in, but if she never goes out and sees anyone she'll just get even more depressed – it's a ....

6. We were stuck behind this big lorry going incredibly slowly for twenty minutes, but we finally managed to .... just before Northampton.

7. I learnt Italian and Spanish easily, but learning Russian is a completely ....

8. I wish you would think more carefully before you opened your mouth to speak! Do you realize how many times you .... this evening?

9. Amanda and Nigel have never met before, so we'll have drinks in the garden before dinner, just to ....

10. I've forgotten Olwen's telephone number again! Give me the telephone directory and I'll ....

11. All of these motorbikes are available for rent, so you can .... Just tell me which one you want when you've decided.

12. Peter asked Kate to .... his bag while he went to ask why the train was late.

In this unit, as you have seen, some of the idiomatic expressions are informal or even very informal, but others can be used in both a formal and an informal context. This exercise gives you practice in choosing the right expression for different contexts.

In each question below, first decide who you think is speaking, or where you would read the item. Then choose from the possibilities in the brackets either the idiomatic expression or the more formal way of saying the same thing. **N.B.** *Although it is often true that formal English is written and informal English spoken, this is not always necessarily true.*

1. 'I really don't mind which chocolate you eat, but please hurry up and (take your pick/select the chocolate of your choice)!'

2. The company is transferring Mr Clanger from the public relations department to a post in personnel. The decision was made as a result of the embarrassment he caused the company by (putting his foot in it/making tactless remarks) during public enquiries into their waste disposal policy.

3. 'John, I've got a new class today. Have you got any good ideas for (breaking the ice/creating a more congenial atmosphere) with them?'

4. 'Was your boss annoyed about losing the contract?'
'Annoyed? He practically (hit the roof/exploded with anger).'

5. 'Aren't you worried about the development of nuclear weapons in the Third World?'
'Of course we are worried, but without further legislation all we can do is to (keep an eye on/monitor) those countries which we know are developing them.'

6. Bad reading is a (vicious circle/self-perpetuating problem). The child who does not read much, reads badly. Consequently he or she does not enjoy reading and so reads less.

7. Many Eastern European countries used to have a controlled economy. Surviving in an open world market is (a different kettle of fish/another matter altogether).

8. 'O.K. I think everyone's here. Shall we (get down to/start) business? What's the first item on the agenda, Bill?'

9. 'It's a bit of a worry going away for so long when there've been so many burglaries recently. Could you (keep an eye on/monitor) the house while we're away?'

10. 'What's wrong? What have I said? Don't tell me I've gone and (put my foot in it/made a tactless remark) again!

Your teacher will give you one or more idioms from this unit to work with. For each idiom, think about a time when you (or someone you know or have heard about) had the experience which this idiom describes.

Prepare some notes, so that you can tell another student about this experience (you can ask your teacher for help with any vocabulary). The important thing is that you mustn't use the idiom when you are talking.

When you have talked about the experience, the other student(s) should be able to produce the idiom, and can then ask you some more questions.

Look at this example for **to look someone up**:

Student A: When my family went to France last year on holiday, we decided to stop in Toulouse and see if we could find an old penfriend, Michelle, who I used to write to. We went to the address I had but there was a completely different family living there.'

Student B: You mean, you decided to *look her up*, but she wasn't there.

Student A: Yes, she'd moved house. But the family had her new address and . . .

Student B: Did you find her?

Student A: Oh yes, she . . .

etc.

1

**'It's no good complaining to me about the smoke,
you're barking at the wrong tree.'**

Dogs normally do bark *at* things. Here you need a preposition
which suggests there is something like a cat above it in the
branches of a tree.

**'It's no good complaining to me about the smoke,
you're ....'**

This expression means that you are trying to find the answer
to a problem but are looking in the wrong place.

This is an informal expression. A formal way of saying the
same thing is *to pursue the wrong line of enquiry*,
e.g. 'The police did not realize that they were pursuing the
wrong line of enquiry until yesterday when new evidence was
presented to them.'

**'Fergus had been engaged for six months, but on
the day of the wedding his feet got cold.'**

You can say that a part of the body has a problem in this
way, e.g. 'Don't go out without an umbrella. Your hair will
get wet', or 'I had to stop sunbathing because my legs were
getting burnt'. In this expression, though, you say that the
person, *not* the part of the body, gets the problem. You still
use the same verb.

'Fergus had been engaged for six months, but on the day of the wedding ....'

We use this expression when we are about to do something which needs courage. But, as the time for doing it gets closer (often it happens at the last moment), we lose the courage.

This is a fairly informal expression. A more formal way of saying the same thing is *to lose one's nerve,*
e.g. 'It is not uncommon for soldiers, when faced with a real enemy for the first time, to lose their nerve and be unable to react as they should.'

3

**'Raffaella was having an argument with her sister
when she suddenly turned me on.'**

It's important where you put the object (*me*) with this phrasal
verb. If you put it between the verb and the preposition, it
means to make someone feel very attracted towards you. For
the right meaning here, put the object after the preposition.

'Raffaella was having an argument with her sister when she suddenly ....'

Here the meaning is to attack someone. You can use it for animals, like dogs, when they physically attack someone. If you use it to describe people, it can mean that they attack someone physically or with words. We often use it with *suddenly* because the attack is unexpected.

The expression is used informally and also fairly formally. A more formal way of saying the same thing is *to attack (suddenly)*,
e.g. Patients suffering from this psychological disorder may appear well-balanced, but will often (suddenly attack) the doctor who is carrying out the interview.

4

**'On the school trip to France, the French teacher
and her husband really lost their faces when the
hotel manager couldn't understand their French.'**

You never use the possessive pronoun (his/her/their, etc) with
this expression, or put any other word between the verb and
the noun. You also never use the plural, even if it is more
than one person you are talking about.

'On the school trip to France, the French teacher and her husband really .... when the hotel manager couldn't understand their French.'

This expression describes what happens to people when others see that they are incompetent in some way. People who do this make mistakes that they shouldn't make. They then have to admit that they are wrong and this can be embarrassing. If you use this expression with *save* instead of *lose*, it means that you do something to avoid being embarrassed. (In this case the teachers could tell the children that the hotel manager speaks a different dialect.)

This is used as an informal and as a fairly formal expression, but if we want to say the same thing very formally, we use *to suffer a humiliation*,
e.g. 'The Police suffered a humiliation in the eyes of the public today when they were forced to admit that they had arrested the wrong man.'

5

'Pam had to fill in one of the teachers who was ill.'

You can say that you are *filling in*, but if you name the person who is unable to work you need another preposition after the word *in*.

THE EQUATION, THEREFORE I[...]

'Pam had to .... one of the teachers who was feeling ill.'

This means to do someone's job for them when they are unable to work. It's usually because that person is ill or late and you do it for a short period – a day, a week. It can also be for a longer period, but it always means the other person is going to come back.

This is an expression which is used informally and fairly formally. A slightly more formal way of saying the same thing is *to take someone's place temporarily*,
e.g. NOTICE TO CUSTOMERS
We would like to advise customers of the North Oxford branch of a change of manager. Miss Hannah will be taking Mr Smith's place temporarily until he recovers from illness.

6

'Richard received the sack for not taking enough care with his work.'

This is an informal expression, so you cannot use *receive*. Instead you need the informal verb which has the same meaning.

'Richard .... for not taking enough care with his work.'

This expression means that you lose your job because your employer is not satisfied with your work or behaviour.

This is an informal expression. To say the same thing in a formal way use *to be dismissed*,
e.g. 'Seven workers were dismissed yesterday from the Rover car factory at Oxford when they were found playing cards during the night shift.'

7

**'Kirsty said she didn't know that cats weren't
allowed in the house, but when the landlord
pointed to the notice in her room she didn't have
any legs to stand on.'**

It's true that you need two legs to stand on, but this
expression means that you don't even have one leg to stand
on, so you use the singular with the indefinite article.

'Kirsty said she didn't know that cats weren't allowed in the house, but when the landlord pointed to the notice in her room she ....'

This means it is no longer possible for you to argue that what you are saying is right. It usually happens because someone produces an argument or evidence which *proves* that you are wrong.

This is an informal expression. If we want to express the same idea in a formal context, we use *to be in an untenable position*, e.g. 'The state prosecutor has produced so much evidence of illegal practices by the bank's directors that their position is now untenable.'

8

**'I tried not to worry about the job interview, but
in the waiting room I had a butterfly in my
stomach.'**

It's true that one butterfly would give you this feeling, but we
always use the plural with this expression.

'I tried not to worry about the job interview, but in the waiting room I had ....'

This expression describes the feeling you get before doing something which you feel worried about. You feel nervous, but it's not always serious enough to stop you doing it. (You don't *have* to say *in your stomach*, because everyone understands where you have this feeling). In the present tense we generally say *I've got* and not *I have*.

This is an informal expression. A formal way of saying the same thing is *to feel apprehensive*, e.g. 'Candidates will often feel very apprehensive before an interview, so it is recommended that interviewers spend a few minutes chatting to them in order to make them feel more relaxed.'

9

**'I was annoyed when the doorbell rang and I had
to answer the door, but it was a blessing in a
disguise.'**

A *disguise* is the thing you wear so that people don't recognise
you (except at parties, where you wear *fancy dress*). In this
expression you don't use an article.

'I was annoyed when the doorbell rang and I had to answer the door, but it was a ....'

A *blessing* here is something good that happens to you. This expression means that something good might at first appear to be something bad. It's only later that you realize that you are glad it happened.

This is a fairly informal expression but there is no simple way to express the same idea formally. The meaning is similar to 'a good thing which seems at first to be a bad thing'.

10

**'Michael was worried about being able to punt,
but he soon got the hang for it.'**

The only time you could use *hang for* is when someone is
punished by hanging for a crime they have committed. Here
you need another preposition.

**'Michael was worried about being able to punt,
but he soon ....'**

This expression means that someone has just learned how to do some new activity. They are not very good at it yet, but they can do it and are getting more confident all the time.

This is an informal expression. A formal way of expressing the same idea is *to become (reasonably) competent at*,
e.g. 'One example of Anatol's genius is that, at the age of four, having watched chess being played just once before, he was, in a matter of minutes, able to become competent at the game.'

PRACTICE

UNIT FOUR

 Decide whether these sentences are right or wrong. If a sentence is wrong, correct it.

1. I don't know why you're showing me your empty chocolate box. You're barking at the wrong tree, because I don't even like chocolate.

2. Chris was very enthusiastic at first about the idea of climbing Mount Snowdon with me, but I think his feet are getting cold now.

3. I never get nervous playing the violin in front of friends, but I do get butterflies in my stomach just before a concert.

4. It was a really good talk on Australian politics, but the speaker certainly lost face when he couldn't answer any of the questions the audience asked him afterwards.

5. Doctor Herdman has had to go home today, so Dr May is filling in for him.

6. If anybody catches you stealing that office equipment, you'll certainly receive the sack.

7. You can't wear your new leather jacket if you're going to tell your dad you need money – you wouldn't have a leg to stand on.

8. I thought the police had come to question Bob, but then they suddenly turned on me and started firing all sorts of difficult questions at me.

9. I was disappointed when Louise couldn't come to the theatre, but as there were only two tickets left when my wife and I got there, it was a blessing in a disguise.

10. You'll find the new word processor a bit strange at first, but don't worry, you'll get the hang for it in a few days.

11. The government is trying to save its face after the disastrous local election results, by saying that it's just a temporary protest vote.

12. One minute the dog was making friendly noises, the next minute it suddenly turned on me.

B *Complete the following sentences using the expressions you have practised in this unit.*

1. Have you heard? The management has said that anyone arriving late more than three times in one week will ....

2. Sandra was really fed up when she missed the last bus from London, but when she heard later on the news that it had crashed on the motorway, she realised it was a ....

3. I'm sorry about charging you the wrong price. I don't actually work here normally – I'm just .... a friend who's away on holiday.

4. Why are you asking us all these questions? Do you think we know anything about the stolen money? I'm afraid you're ....

5. I love it when you wear that perfume. It really .... !

6. I wouldn't say I was exactly frightened of flying, but I do .... just before the plane takes off.

7. We didn't believe him when he said after the concert that he was feeling ill. It seemed like he was just trying to .... after playing so badly.

8. It looks so easy to ski, but it took me about two weeks to really ....

9. Both Michael and Ray had agreed to do the parachute jump with us, but Michael .... at the last minute and decided not to come.

10. Sally thought that Ralph was incredibly nice and friendly, and then one day he suddenly .... and started accusing her of all sorts of terrible things.

11. We all make mistakes sometimes. You'll just have to be prepared to .... and tell your class that you taught them the wrong lesson.

12. Jonathan kept saying that he was sure that Freud was German, but when I showed him the encyclopaedia, which stated clearly that he was born in Austria, he didn't ....

In this unit, as you have seen, some of the idiomatic expressions are informal or even very informal, but others can be used in both a formal and an informal context. This exercise gives you practice in choosing the right expression for different contexts.

In each question below, first decide who you think is speaking, or where you would read the item. Then choose from the possibilities in the brackets either the idiomatic expression or the more formal way of saying the same thing. N.B. Although it is often true that formal English is written and informal English spoken, this is not always necessarily true.

1. 'Mr Harvey, I understand that you (got the sack/were dismissed) from your last place of employment. Could you explain to the court why this was?'

2. 'Are you all right, Jane? You look pale.'
'Well, to be honest, Dave, I ('ve got butterflies in my stomach/feel very apprehensive). You see, I've got my driving test this afternoon.'

3. 'Don't try to pretend you weren't in the pub last night, because (you don't have a leg to stand on/your position is untenable). You see, I saw you coming out of there with my own eyes, at about eleven o'clock.'

4. Having examined Mr Griffith's dog, I would say it was docile and would judge it unlikely that it would (turn on/suddenly attack) a complete stranger without provocation.

5. Plato thought that, in refusing to believe in the possibility of real knowledge, many of his contemporaries were (barking up the wrong tree/pursuing the wrong line of enquiry).

6. Due to the president's illness, the Vice-President will be (filling in for him/taking his place temporarily) at the United Nations conference in Geneva.

7. The course lasts six days, and although this is clearly not long enough to become an expert computer programmer, trainees will find that, after this time, they (have got the hang of/are reasonably competent at) it.

8. 'Come on, Sally, let's go home. It's getting late and mum said we had to be back by seven.'
'No, I want to explore this old house. You wanted to too earlier. What's the matter? Are you (getting cold feet/losing your nerve) now?'

9. 'Look, you'll have to forgive her, if you want her back.'
'I can't. She's made a fool of me.'
'Well, you must decide which is more important to you – not
(losing face/suffering a humiliation) or having her back.'

10. 'It's your first day, Jane, so there's no need to get upset if things
start going wrong. You'll soon (get the hang of/become competent
at) the job, don't worry.'

 *Your teacher will give you one or more idioms from this unit
to work with. For each idiom, think about a time when you
(or someone you know or have heard about) had the
experience which this idiom describes.*

*Prepare some notes, so that you can tell another student
about this experience (you can ask your teacher for help
with any vocabulary). The important thing is that you
mustn't use the idiom when you are talking.*

*When you have talked about the experience, the other
student(s) should be able to produce the idiom, and they can
then ask you some more questions.*

Look at this example for the idiom **to have butterflies**.

Student A: I belong to the local drama group in my town and last
year I had quite a big part in the play we were doing. It
was the first time I'd had such a big part and I had a lot
of lines to learn, but I really enjoyed it and everyone said
I was very good during the rehearsals. I was actually
looking forward to performing the play in public, but on
the first night I suddenly got very frightened before the
performance.

Student B: You mean you *had butterflies in your stomach?*

Student A: Yes! I had them really badly!

Student B: And how did the play go?

Student A: It went well after the first few minutes.

Student B: Were you still nervous?

Student A: No, I was too busy thinking about my lines.

Student B: What was the play . . . ?

etc.

1

**'I hear that John fell head over feet in love on his
skiing holiday.'**

Instead of *feet*, you have to use a word here for a *part* of your
foot. It's the part right at the back of your foot, and it's the
same word that we use for the thick piece of rubber or leather
at the back of your shoe. It's always in the plural in this
expression.

'I hear that John .... on his skiing holiday.'

When a romance begins, we say you *fall* in love. If you fall in love as much as this expression suggests, then you completely lose control of your emotions. It might be a good or a bad thing!

This is an informal expression. If you want to say the same thing in a less informal way, the expression is similar, *to fall hopelessly in love,*
e.g. 'It is said that when the two first met at the Royal Opera House in London last May, they fell hopelessly in love.'

2

'Kath said she had some bones to pick with David.'

There could be more than one problem to talk about when you use this expression, but in fact we always use it in the singular.

'Kath said she had .... with David.'

This expression means that you are angry about something another person has done and that you are now going to talk to them about it. You often use it to warn someone that you, or another person, are going to accuse them of something they did earlier, which you have now remembered. In the present tense you usually say *I've got* rather than *I have*.

This is an informal expression. A formal way of saying the same thing is *a grievance to discuss*, e.g. 'If you have a grievance to discuss with the management, you should follow the proper procedures for this. A complaints box is to be found on each floor of the building, where your particular grievance can be posted.'

3

**'It wasn't easy to paint the living room ceiling,
but my father gave me his hand.'**

With this expression you never use the possessive pronoun
his/her/their/my, etc. You just use the indefinite article. Also,
you never use the plural of *hand*, even when you are talking
about more than one person.

**'It wasn't easy to paint the living room ceiling,
but my father ....'**

This means to help someone to do something when they are
finding it difficult to do on their own. It's usually not a very
long or difficult job (e.g. carrying a suitcase for someone,
moving a table, etc.) and if you help it could be done quite
quickly. (When people use this expression to ask for help, they
sometimes use *lend* instead of *give*.)

This is an informal expression. A formal way of saying the
same thing is *to assist*,
e.g. 'If you have any difficulty carrying your purchases to the
car, one of our staff is always on duty to assist you.'

4

**'I don't know why Alan made a molehill into a
mountain. It was only a small stain.'**

In English there are two ways of creating one thing from
another. We can either 'make X *into* Y' or we can 'make Y *out
of* X'. Here you need the second way.

**'I don't know why Alan made .... It was
only a small stain.'**

We use this expression when someone treats something as
much worse or much more serious than it really is.

This is an informal expression. A formal way of saying the
same thing is *to exaggerate the seriousness/difficulty of (something)*,
e.g. 'To say that our company's current financial problems
constitute a crisis would be to exaggerate the seriousness of
the situation.'

5

'My landlady has a little dog that drives me into the wall.'

You can drive a car into a wall, but the verb *drive* in this expression doesn't mean what you do in a car. To get the right meaning here, you need to change the preposition, so that you are going in the same direction as the wall is.

'My landlady has a little dog that ....'

Drive in this sense means to *push* or *send* just as in the past cowboys on horses used to *drive* the cows in front of them. This expression means that something or someone makes you so angry that it sends you crazy.

This is an informal and colloquial expression. To express the same idea in a formal way use *to irritate intensely*, e.g. 'As a king he was much loved and respected by his people, but he had one habit which irritated those around him intensely. This was his inability to take advice from others.'

6

**'The Spanish boy I met on holiday three years ago
still drops me some lines sometimes.'**

You often talk about writing or reading *lines* when you mean
that it's a small amount, e.g. 'At the end of the letter I
managed to write a few lines in French'. However, in this
expression you have to use the singular form.

**'The Spanish boy I met on holiday three years ago
still .... sometimes.'**

This means to write a fairly short letter to a friend or someone
you know quite well. You don't write a lot or tell them very
personal things in a letter like this. It's something you do
occasionally because you don't want to lose contact with them
completely. It's also a popular way of asking someone to write
to you when they go away.

This is an informal expression. A formal way of expressing a
similar idea is *to write (to . . .)*,
e.g. 'I will ask Mr Robbins to write to you to confirm the
appointment.'

7

**'I didn't think my drawing of Masami was right,
so I decided to start again from the scratch.'**

You would normally use an article with the noun *scratch*, but
in this expression you don't need one.

**'I didn't think my drawing of Masami was right,
so I decided to ....'**

This expression means that you start something from the very
beginning. You could use it about a business or some other
activity when you begin with nothing and do everything
yourself. If you make mistakes when you are doing something
and too much has gone wrong for you to correct, it is often
easier to start again from the very beginning, as in
this example.

This is an informal expression. A formal way of saying the
same thing is *to start afresh,*
e.g. 'When the authors were asked to produce a new English
dictionary, they decided, rather than simply revising the old
edition, to start afresh with the whole project.'

8

'If I had the chance to sleep in the tent, I'd jump on it.'

You normally jump *on* something but then it's not a phrasal verb with an idiomatic meaning. You need another preposition to give you the idiomatic meaning.

**'If I had the chance to sleep in the tent, I'd
....'**

This phrasal verb is always followed by *the chance, the opportunity*, or *it*. It means that you would be very quick to take this chance or opportunity if it came to you.

This is an informal expression. The formal way of expressing the same idea is *to seize the opportunity*,
e.g. 'The President would have seized the opportunity to engage in peace talks. However, the other protagonists in the dispute refused to negotiate and in May 1957 civil war broke out in the country.'

9

'You must get off that parcel soon, otherwise it won't arrive by Christmas.'

The position of the object is important here. To *get off* something is the opposite of to *get on*, e.g. 'Get off that bed with your dirty shoes!' or 'You get off the bus in the High Street'. For the meaning you want here, put the object between the verb and the preposition.

'You must .... soon, otherwise it won't arrive by Christmas.'

You can use this phrasal verb to talk about letters or parcels. It means *to post* them. It is often used after *must* when you should have posted them some time before. You can also use it without any object to talk about a person. Then it means that the person needs to leave very soon, e.g. 'Is it 10.30? I really must get off!'

This expression is informal. Another way of saying the same thing either informally or formally is . . . *to send*, e.g. 'The British Telecom share offer closes at 12 p.m. tomorrow. If you are still interested in applying for shares, complete the form below and send it to the above address.'

10

**'I was worried about the condition of the ship's
bathroom, but Henry told me that was just the top
of the iceberg.'**

To describe the very top of an iceberg you use another similar
word. It's actually the same word you use for the very end of
your finger, toes, nose and tongue (see page 10).

'I was worried about the condition of the ship's bathroom, but Henry told me that was just ....'

Most of an iceberg is under the water, so the bit you see is only a very small part of it. We use this expression to say that the problem you know about is in fact a small part of a much bigger problem.

This expression is used both formally and informally. The meaning is similar to 'a small part of a much bigger problem'.

PRACTICE

UNIT FIVE

 Decide whether these sentences are right or wrong. If a sentence is wrong, correct it.

1. It's wonderful to fall head over feet in love, but you should remember that it can't last forever.

2. Sue wants to see you, James, and she doesn't look very pleased. I think she's got a bone to pick with you.

3. Could you lend me a hand with this table? It's incredibly heavy.

4. I don't think you need have any doubts about whether Sarah would want to come hot-air ballooning – I know she'd jump on the chance.

5. It doesn't matter that much if you're a bit late for work. I do think you're making a molehill out of a mountain.

6. If you have time, do drop me some lines when you're in South America.

7. After losing all his money in business and having to sell his house, Martin decided to move to Australia and start from scratch.

8. I wish the girl next door would stop playing that rap music – it's driving me into the wall.

9. I'll call at the post office and try to get these letters off.

10. Customs officials seized eight tonnes of cocaine at Heathrow Airport last year, but they say this is just the tip of the iceberg.

11. Yoshie is going to be at work later than she thought, but she hopes to get off by about 8 o'clock.

12. This work must be finished by tonight. Lend me your hand, would you?

B *Complete the following sentences using the expressions you have practised in this unit.*

1. If you could write a quick reply to Helge's letter, I could .... to him this afternoon.

2. Nicky doesn't phone us from New Zealand because it's too expensive, but she .... fairly often, just to say how she is.

3. Reports suggest that 5% of customers were unhappy with their package holidays last year, but as many people don't actually make an official complaint, this may be just ....

4. I hate washing up, but if you need any help, I'll .... with the cooking.

5. There's no need to be so angry. It's only a glass I broke! You're making ....

6. As soon as Doris and Kevin met, they .... They got married six months later.

7. Ah! Dave, there you are! I've got .... you! It's about that photography book you gave me back yesterday. Was it you or one of your children that decided to use it as a drawing book?

8. If the train stops at Radley, you could .... there and walk to my house.

9. Oh no! Someone switched the computer off while I was out, and I hadn't saved any of the text I was writing. Now I'll have to ....

10. I'd .... to work in France for a year if someone offered it to me. I really need to practise my French.

11. I'm sorry I shouted at your little boy, I didn't mean to. He just kept asking 'Why? Why? Why?' after everything I said, and it was ....

12. The coach was supposed to leave at 7.30, but Mick Parsley was late and we finally .... at 8.15.

In this unit, as you have seen, most of the idiomatic expressions are informal or even very informal, but others can be used in both a formal and an informal context. This exercise gives you practice in choosing the right expression for different contexts.

In each question below, first decide who you think is speaking, or where you would read the item. Then choose from the possibilities in the brackets either the idiomatic expression or the more formal way of saying the same thing. N.B. Although it is often true that formal English is written and informal English spoken, this is not always necessarily true.

1. 'The news of their forthcoming marriage is a matter of no small wonder to me, Mrs Musgrove. Indeed, I was not in the least aware that they had fallen so (head over heels/hopelessly) in love with each other, until you yourself informed me of the fact.'

2. 'Hey, I've got (a bone to pick/a grievance to discuss) with you. Why did you tell me that the brakes on this bike worked? I almost killed myself yesterday!'

3. Three men were actually seen leaving the bank, but it is believed that a fourth man (gave them a hand/assisted them) with the robbery.

4. 'There's just one more point I'd like to make, which concerns the so called "flood" of refugees now coming into this country. It seems to me that, with only 570 refugees being admitted last year, the government is (making a mountain out of a molehill/exaggerating the seriousness of the problem).'

5. 'And could you also telephone Miss Briggs and inform her that her application for the secretarial post is being considered and that we will (drop her a line/write to her) as soon as a decision has been made.'

6. Dear Mr Conway,
   Thank you for your letter inviting me to come and visit your school on 23 January. An 11.00 a.m. appointment would be suitable for me, but as I will need to (get off/leave) by 12.00 noon, perhaps I should come earlier. Please let me know if this would be convenient.

7. 'As your requirements for the building have been considerably revised, the original plans no longer seem appropriate. We feel it would now be better to (start from scratch/start afresh) and commission a new set of plans from one of our architects.'

8. 'You're mad if you don't take that job in Jamaica. If I was offered a job like that, I'd (jump at the chance/seize the opportunity).'

9. It is difficult to believe that such a small insect could have any effect on an animal so large and thick-skinned as a buffalo, but in fact they are (driven up the wall/irritated intensely) by the constant attentions of these flies.

10. I can only apologize for the delay in completing work on your computer program and assure you that we will (get it off/send it) to you as soon as it is ready.

Your teacher will give you one or more idioms from this unit to work with. For each idiom, think about a time when you (or someone you know or have heard about) had the experience which this idiom describes.

Prepare some notes, so that you can tell another student about this experience (you can ask your teacher for help with any vocabulary). The important thing is that you **mustn't use the idiom** *when you are talking.*

When you have talked about the experience, the other student(s) should be able to produce the idiom, and can then ask you some more questions.

Look at this example for **to fall head over heels in love**:

Student A: I had a party at my house last year and invited some friends from the university where I study. My brother is 4 years older than me and most of my friends, but he decided to join the party. He spent the whole evening talking to a girl who does the same course as me, but I didn't know her very well then. In fact I got to know her extremely well, because she spent most of the summer holidays at my house, because she and my brother couldn't be separated!

Student B: They obviously *fell head over heels in love.*

Student A: Yes, absolutely.

Student B: Is she still his girlfriend?

Student A: No. They broke up last month.

Student B: Oh. What happened?

Student A: Well, he . . .
  etc.

ANSWERS

The number in brackets at the end of the practice sentences refers to the page where you will find the correct explanation.

Unit One

1. Mr and Mrs Doubleday are not very good parents – they never <u>put their foot down.</u>
2. Valerie's new boyfriend is definitely in love with her – <u>he gives her a ring</u> every evening.
3. Clare can't <u>put up with</u> Ashley's motorbike any longer – it's too noisy.
4. Dave and Helen managed to reach the theatre before the opera started, but it was <u>a race against time.</u>
5. I couldn't remember his name when he arrived, but it was <u>on the tip of my tongue.</u>
6. We keep trying to find time to visit you, but we <u>are tied up with the dogs</u> most evenings.
7. When the new cook started work, Maurizio was always <u>pulling his leg.</u>
8. I arrived twenty minutes after the film had started, but Richard soon <u>put me in the picture.</u>
9. The doctor could see that James was <u>full of beans</u> when he came for the medical examination.
10. It's sad that so many animals are <u>run over</u> by cars these days.

Practice – 1A

1. RIGHT. (p. 2)
2. WRONG – If I manage to get tickets for the concert tonight, I'll <u>give you a ring</u> and let you know. (p. 4)
3. WRONG – I don't know how Astrid can put up <u>with</u> the noise of the traffic all day. (p. 6)
4. RIGHT. (p. 8)
5. WRONG – Oh, I wish I could remember the name of that village we stayed in. It's on the <u>tip</u> of my tongue. (p. 10)
6. RIGHT. (p. 12)

7. WRONG—Pam, don't look so worried. Roger's only pulling your leg. (p. 14)

8. WRONG—Well, I hope you had a good holiday. We've been having problems with our agent in Paris while you've been away, but Colin will put you in the picture about it all. (p. 16)

9. WRONG—Kate is full of beans today. Is her boyfriend back from abroad? (p. 18)

10. RIGHT. (p. 20)

11. RIGHT. (p. 5)

12. RIGHT. (p. 19)

Practice – 1B

1. pulling my leg (p. 14) *2.* put up with (p. 6) *3.* give her a ring (p. 4) *4.* tied up with (p. 12) *5.* full of beans (p. 18) *6.* run over (p. 20) *7.* put our foot down (p. 2) *8.* tip of my tongue (p. 10) *9.* race against time (p. 8) *10.* put you in the picture (p. 16) *11.* put you up (p. 5) *12.* overrun (p. 9)

Practice – 1C

1. A news report. (full of beans/in high spirits) (p. 18)

2. A telephone answering machine for the Electricity Board. (give you a ring/telephone you) (p. 4)

3. Information sent to participants of a conference. (put participants up/provide accommodation for participants) (p. 5)

4. Two people who share a house together, talking. (put my foot down/assert my authority) (p. 2)

5. Television or radio news. (run over/hit) (p. 20)

6. A history book. (put the reader in the picture about/explain to the reader the background to) (p. 16)

7. A doctor's receptionist speaking to a patient on the telephone. (tied up with/occupied with) (p. 12)

8. Two people who share a house talking. It could also be in a very informal place of work. (put up with/tolerate) (p. 6)

9. A friend or relative talking. (His name has been on the tip of my tongue/I haven't quite been able to remember his name) (p. 10)
10. Diane's friend or relative talking on the telephone. (put me up/provide accommodation for me) (p. 5)

Practice – 1D

Open answers.

Unit Two

1. He was worried before the exam, but for him it was a piece of cake.
2. It takes Bill a long time to show his holiday slides – he keeps getting carried away.
3. When Philippa was decorating her house she broke her arm, but she was lucky to have friends she could fall back on.
4. I see that Mr and Mrs Davis have finally met their match on the tennis court.
5. Mrs Johnson said she was glad to see the back of Karl.
6. Paul will have to come back down to earth one day.
7. This music takes me back to the time I spent in Greece.
8. Don't worry about Sharon and Wayne arguing – it's just a storm in a teacup.
9. The only trouble with teaching that class is Marcel – he's always splitting hairs.
10. I ran into Giles in town yesterday. It was great to see him again.

Practice – 2A

1. RIGHT. (p. 26)
2. WRONG — Please have some more soup. There was only supposed to be enough for four people, but I got carried away when I was making it. (p. 28)
3. RIGHT. (p. 30)

4. WRONG—I didn't think anyone else could eat as much as I do, but we certainly met our <u>match</u> in Pat and Jack. (p. 32)

5. WRONG—Paul has had so many problems with that car — he'll be glad to see <u>the back of it.</u> (p. 34)

6. RIGHT. (p. 36)

7. RIGHT. (p. 38)

8. RIGHT. (p. 40)

9. RIGHT. (p. 42)

10. WRONG—I hope I don't run <u>into</u> Paul if I go into town. I owe him £10. (p. 44)

11. RIGHT. (p. 27)

12. WRONG—I'm sorry about your car. I'm afraid I ran <u>into</u> a tree at the end of the road. (If you hit a tree when you're in a car, it wouldn't go *under* the wheels.) (p. 44)

Practice – 2B

1. splitting hairs (p. 42) *2.* get carried away (p. 28) *3.* come (back) down to earth (p. 36) *4.* fall back on (p. 30) *5.* meet his match (p. 32) *6.* ran into (p. 44) *7.* takes me back to (p. 38) *8.* storm in a teacup (p. 40) *9.* see the back of (p. 34) *10.* a piece of cake (p. 26) *11.* ran over (p. 43) *12.* ran into (p. 44)

Practice – 2C

1. An interview or appointment in a company office. (a piece of cake/<u>very easy</u>) (p. 26)

2. A job reference. (get carried away/<u>be overenthusiastic</u>) (p. 28)

3. A notice in a building. (to fall back on/<u>to rely on in case of need</u>) (p. 30)

4. A sports report, either on TV or radio. (<u>met his match</u>/found an equal) (p. 32)

5. An interview with a top politician. (glad to see the back of him/<u>relieved that he has left</u>) (p. 34)

6. A speech by a politician or an employer. (come back down to earth/<u>accept reality</u>) (p. 36)

7. A married couple talking. (<u>take you back to</u>/evoke memories of) (p. 38)

8. A news report. (a storm in a teacup/<u>an unnecessary commotion</u>) (p. 40)

9. Two friends or students talking. (<u>split hairs</u>/be pedantic) (p. 42)

10. A news report. (ran into each other/<u>met by chance</u>) (p. 44)

Practice – 2D

Open answers.

Unit Three

1. I haven't seen Jimmy for ages. Next time I'm in Scotland I must <u>look him up.</u>

2. When we got to the holiday homes, the manager told us to <u>take our pick.</u>

3. I'll have to lose some weight because this is becoming <u>a vicious circle.</u>

4. I'd forgotten that Mrs Matthews' sister died last month, so when I asked who the photograph was of, I really <u>put my foot in it.</u>

5. Geoff and Jude usually organize a few games to <u>break the ice</u> at their parties.

6. Mr Sturgess is going to <u>take over</u> Mr Simpson's position as manager.

7. I learnt how to make Turkish coffee quite easily, but making an Italian espresso was a completely <u>different kettle of fish.</u>

8. My brother <u>hit the roof</u> when I told him that I'd crashed his car.

9. It was nearly 9.20 a.m., but only one person in the office had <u>got down to</u> work.

10. Can you <u>keep an eye on</u> the soup? I'm just going to make a phone call.

Practice – 3A

1. RIGHT. (p. 50)

2. WRONG — We prefer to buy vegetables from the supermarket, because then we can take our <u>pick</u>. (p. 52)

3. WRONG — Heroin users become more and more unhappy, and then need more of the drug to make them happy, so it becomes a vicious <u>circle</u>. (p. 54)

4. WRONG — Do you think I put my foot <u>in</u> it when I asked Rosie if she'd bought the cake from a shop? (p. 56)

5. RIGHT. (p. 58)

6. RIGHT. (p. 60)

7. WRONG — I thought the fact that I used to play the piano might help, but learning to play the piano is a different kettle of <u>fish</u> altogether. (p. 62)

8. RIGHT. (p. 64)

9. WRONG — I've been sitting and reading the newspaper all morning. I just can't seem to get down <u>to</u> work. (p. 66)

10. WRONG — Harriet asked Peter to keep <u>an</u> eye on Robert and Eli while she went to the shop to get them an ice-cream. (p. 68)

11. RIGHT. (p. 49)

12. WRONG — '. . . and as they come round the corner into the last 200 metres, Rogers is <u>overtaking</u> the Kenyan runner in the outside lane.' (p. 59)

Practice – 3B

1. look you up (p. 50)   *2.* taking over (p. 60)   *3.* hit the roof (p. 64)
4. get down to (p. 66)   *5.* vicious circle (p. 54)   *6.* overtake it (p. 59)
7. different kettle of fish (p. 62)   *8.* put your foot in it (p. 56)
9. break the ice (p. 58)   *10.* look it up (p. 49)   *11.* take your pick
(p. 52)   *12.* keep an eye on (p. 68)

Practice – 3C

1. A friend or relative talking. (<u>take your pick</u>/select the chocolate of your choice) (p. 52)

2. A company memo. (putting his foot in it/<u>making tactless remarks</u>) (p. 56)

3. A teacher talking to a colleague. (<u>breaking the ice</u>/creating a more congenial atmosphere) (p. 58)

4. A friend or relative talking. (<u>hit the roof</u>/exploded with anger) (p. 64)

5. Interview with a politician or diplomat. (keep an eye on/<u>monitor</u>) (p. 68)

6. An article in a book, magazine or newspaper, about education. (<u>vicious circle</u>/self-perpetuating problem) (p. 54) 'Self-perpetuating problem' is also possible here, as the style is formal.

7. An article in a book, magazine or newspaper, about education. (a different kettle of fish/<u>another matter altogether</u>) (p. 62)

8. A fairly informal meeting between people who know each other well. (<u>get down to</u>/start) 'Start' is a possible answer here, but 'get down to' sounds better with the informal style of the language. (p. 66)

9. A neighbour talking to another neighbour. (<u>keep an eye on</u>/monitor) (p. 68)

10. A friend or relative talking. (<u>put my foot in it</u>/ made a tactless remark) (p. 56)

Practice – 3D

Open answers.

Unit Four

1. It's no good complaining to me about the smoke, you're <u>barking up the wrong tree.</u>

2. Fergus had been engaged for six months, but on the day of the wedding <u>he got cold feet.</u>

3. Raffaella was having an argument with her sister when she suddenly <u>turned on me.</u>

4. On the school trip to France, the French teacher and her

husband really <u>lost face</u> when the hotel manager couldn't understand their French.

5. Pam had to <u>fill in for</u> one of the teachers who was feeling ill.
6. Richard <u>got the sack</u> for not taking enough care with his work.
7. Kirsty said she didn't know that cats weren't allowed in the house, but when the landlord pointed to the notice in her room she <u>didn't have a leg to stand on.</u>
8. I tried not to worry about the job interview, but in the waiting room I had <u>butterflies in my stomach.</u>
9. I was annoyed when the doorbell rang and I had to answer the door, but it was a <u>blessing in disguise.</u>
10. Michael was worried about being able to punt, but he soon <u>got the hang of it.</u>

Practice – 4A

1. WRONG — I don't know why you're showing me your empty chocolate box. You're barking <u>up</u> the wrong tree, because I don't even like chocolate. (p. 74)
2. WRONG — Chris was very enthusiastic at first about the idea of climbing Mount Snowdon with me, but I think <u>he's getting cold feet</u> now. (p. 76)
3. RIGHT. (p. 78)
4. RIGHT. (p. 80)
5. RIGHT. (p. 82)
6. WRONG — If anyone catches you stealing that office equipment, you'll certainly <u>get</u> the sack. (p. 84)
7. RIGHT. (p. 86)
8. RIGHT. (p. 88)
9. WRONG — I was disappointed when Louise couldn't come to the theatre, but there were only two tickets left when my wife and I got there, so it was a blessing <u>in disguise.</u> (p. 90)
10. WRONG — You'll find the new word processor a bit strange at first, but don't worry, you'll get the hang <u>of</u> it in a few days. (p. 92)
11. RIGHT. (p. 80)
12. RIGHT. (p. 78)

Practice – 4B

1. get the sack (p. 84)   *2.* blessing in disguise (p. 90)   *3.* filling in for (p. 82)   *4.* barking up the wrong tree (p. 74)   *5.* turns me on (p. 77)   *6.* get butterflies (p. 88)   *7.* save face (p. 80)   *8.* get the hang of it (p. 92)   *9.* got cold feet (p. 76)   *10.* turned on her (p. 78)   *11.* lose face (p. 80)   *12.* have a leg to stand on (p. 86)

Practice – 4C

1. A solicitor or barrister speaking in a courtroom. (got the sack/<u>were dismissed</u>) (p. 84)

2. Two friends talking. (<u>'ve got butterflies in my stomach</u>/feel very apprehensive) (p. 88)

3. A friend or relative talking. (<u>you don't have a leg to stand on</u>/your position is untenable) (p. 86)

4. A veterinary surgeon's (vet's) report. (turn on/<u>suddenly attack</u>) (p. 78) 'Turn on' would also be possible as it can be used formally.

5. A book or article on philosophy. (barking up the wrong tree/<u>pursuing the wrong line of enquiry</u>) (p. 74)

6. A statement from the President's office, or a news report. (filling in for him/<u>taking his place temporarily</u>) (p. 82)

7. A brochure or leaflet giving information about training courses. (have got the hang of/<u>are reasonably competent at</u>) (p. 92)

8. Two children talking. (<u>getting cold feet</u>/losing your nerve) (p. 76)

9. Two friends talking. (<u>losing face</u>/suffering a humiliation) (p. 80)

10. An older woman talking to a woman who has just started work. (<u>get the hang of</u>/become competent at) (p. 92)

Practice – 4D

Open answers.

Unit Five

1. I hear that John <u>fell head over heels in love</u> on his skiing holiday.
2. Kath said she had <u>a bone to pick</u> with David.
3. It wasn't easy to paint the living room ceiling, but my father <u>gave me a hand.</u>
4. I don't know why Alan made <u>a mountain out of a molehill.</u> It was only a small stain.
5. My landlady has a little dog that <u>drives me up the wall.</u>
6. The Spanish boy I met on holiday three years ago still <u>drops me a line</u> sometimes.
7. I didn't think my drawing of Masami was right, so I decided to <u>start from scratch.</u>
8. If I had the chance to sleep in the tent, I'<u>d jump at it.</u>
9. You must <u>get that parcel off</u> soon, otherwise it won't arrive by Christmas.
10. I was worried about the condition of the ship's bathroom, but Henry told me that was just <u>the tip of the iceberg.</u>

Practice – 5A

1. WRONG – It's wonderful to fall head over <u>heels</u> in love, but you should remember that it can't last forever. (p. 98)
2. RIGHT. (p. 100)
3. RIGHT. (p. 102)
4. WRONG – I don't think you need have any doubts about whether Sarah would want to come hot-air ballooning – I know she'd jump <u>at</u> the chance. (p. 112)
5. WRONG – It doesn't matter that much if you're a bit late for work. I do think you're making a <u>mountain</u> out of a <u>molehill.</u> (p. 104)
6. WRONG – If you have time, do drop me <u>a line</u> when you're in South America. (p. 108)
7. RIGHT. (p. 110)

8. WRONG—I wish the girl next door would stop playing that rap music – it's driving me <u>up</u> the wall. (p. 106)

9. RIGHT. (p. 114)

10. RIGHT. (p. 116)

11. RIGHT. (p. 114)

12. WRONG—This work must be finished by tonight. Lend me <u>a</u> hand, would you? (p. 102)

Practice – 5B

1. get it off (p. 114)   *2.* drops us a line (p. 108)   *3.* the tip of the iceberg (p. 116)   *4.* give you a hand (p. 102)   *5.* a mountain out of a molehill (p. 104)   *6.* fell head over heels in love (p. 98)   *7.* a bone to pick with (p. 100)   *8.* get off (p. 113)   *9.* start from scratch (p. 110)   *10.* jump at the chance (p. 112)   *11.* driving me up the wall (p. 106)   *12.* got off (p. 114)

Practice – 5C

1. From a novel, probably set in the last century or early this century. (head over heels/<u>hopelessly</u>) (p. 98)

2. A friend or relative talking. (<u>a bone to pick</u>/a grievance to discuss) (p. 100)

3. A news report. (gave them a hand/<u>assisted them</u>) (p. 102)

4. A public talk on a political matter. (making a mountain out of a molehill/<u>exaggerating the seriousness of the problem</u>) (p. 104)

5. A manager talking to a secretary. (drop her a line/<u>write to her</u>) (p. 102)

6. A letter to a principal of a school (get off/<u>leave</u>) (p. 114)

7. A letter from a firm of architects to a client. (start from scratch/<u>start afresh</u>) (p. 110)

8. A friend or relative talking. (<u>jump at the chance</u>/seize the opportunity) (p. 112)

9. From a book or article about wildlife. (driven up the wall/<u>irritated intensely</u>) (p. 106)

10. A letter from a computer company to a client. (get it off/<u>send it</u>) (p. 114)

Practice – 5D

Open answers.

INDEX OF IDIOMS

The definitions given here are meant to help you remember the meaning of the idioms. They are not, and in some cases cannot give, exactly the same meaning as the idioms themselves.

UNIT ONE

UNIT TWO

UNIT THREE

1. To look someone up — *to visit someone you haven't seen for a long time* (p. 50)
2. To take one's pick — *to select the (thing) of your choice* (p. 52)
3. A vicious circle — *a self-perpetuating problem* (p. 54)
4. To put one's foot in it — *to make a tactless remark* (p. 56)
5. To break the ice — *to create a more congenial atmosphere* (p. 58)
6. To take over (from someone) — *to replace someone* (p. 60)
7. A (completely) different kettle of fish (altogether) — *another matter altogether* (p. 62)
8. To hit the roof — *to explode with anger* (p. 64)
9. To get down to — *to start (work of some kind)* (p. 66)
10. To keep an eye on — *to monitor* (p. 68)

UNIT FOUR

1. To bark up the wrong tree — *to pursue the wrong line of enquiry* (p. 74)
2. To get cold feet — *to lose one's nerve* (p. 76)
3. To turn on someone — *to attack (suddenly)* (p. 78)
4. To lose face — *to suffer a humiliation* (p. 80)
5. To fill in for — *to take someone's place temporarily* (p. 82)
6. To get the sack — *to be dismissed from one's job* (p. 84)
7. Not to have a leg to stand on — *to be in an untenable position* (p 86)
8. To have butterflies in your stomach — *to feel apprehensive* (p. 88)
9. A blessing in disguise — *a good thing which seems at first to be a bad thing* (p. 90)
10. To get the hang of — *to become (reasonably) competent at* (p. 92)

UNIT FIVE

1. To fall head over heels in love — *to fall completely in love* (p. 98)
2. To have a bone to pick with someone — *to have a grievance to discuss (with someone)* (p. 100)
3. To give someone a hand — *to assist* (p. 102)

4. To make a mountain out of a molehill — *to exaggerate the seriousness/difficulty of (something)* (p. 104)

5. To drive up the wall — *to irritate intensely* (p. 106)

6. To drop someone a line — *to write to (someone)* (p. 108)

7. To start from scratch — *to start afresh* (p. 110)

8. To jump at the chance — *to seize the opportunity* (p. 112)

9. To get something off — *to send (by post)* (p. 114)

10. The tip of the iceberg — *a small part of a much bigger problem* (p. 116)